PLUM UNDER WRAPS

Akanksha Shrivastava

QUICK READS

by Writersgram Publications

PLUM UNDER WRAPS

Poetry by Akanksha Shrivastava

First Impression: February 2020

ISBN: 978-9389244519

Published by: Writersgram Publications, New Delhi
Imprint: Quick Reads

www.writersgram.com
publications@writersgram.com

Akanksha Shrivastava asserts the moral right to be identified as the author of this book.

CONTENTS

It's you...8

That's why I wonder you say..9

Stand a little more...10

I am afraid to close my eyes...11

I stayed up all night 12

It will all be Okay! 13

What if ?...14

Say Cheese! 15

Your set of mistakes 16

City that never sleeps..17

Love stays 18

Your day awaits 19

Drunk enough ? 20

Isn't it selfish ? 21

Getting lost in the maze 22

Fly Away 23

Better walk away 24

You are suffocating 25

Dear caretaker 26

Living for you 27

Finding love 28

Fear of falling down...29

Slow Poison...30

Building Home 31

Bravest Battles 32

Choice of happiness 33

Homesick 34

Echo of silence...35

The Jar theory...36

Let them be 37

Bring me back 38

Stubborn Child 39

Tiny drops of rain 40

Well then, I like you too 41

Last Love...42

Stories, faces won't tell 43

The Sky is Pink 44

Calculated love 45

Don't want to belong...46

Not alone!...47

Welcome sadness..48

For those eyes 49

You are alive 50

She is a mystery...51

Let's not just talk today 52

Tick tock tick tock 53

Knock knock...54

And then… 55

I feel like I'm Home 56

Should have not..58

A Place 59

A WORD FROM THE AUTHOR

This book is a collection of poems written by me, depicting regular ups and downs faced in my life. Often we think that sharing what we feel deep inside with people in our life may lessen the purity of that emotion. As they may listen and leave it there just like any other story. And so I decided to pen down each and every high tide I faced during multiple situations. Many of them may look relatable to you, As we all have been there, we all have faced the same. Hope you find a little of your thoughts weaved in here, And I will be glad if you can say, "Oh I've been there!"

Just remember these words,

"Oh Dear!
One day you may want to run away from wherever you are, straight to your home. And that time maybe, you won't feel like Home anymore."

Akanksha Shrivastava

IT'S YOU

It's not okay to judge someone
To judge them by their looks.
But what if it's you only
Judging yourself every second.

It's you only body shaming yourself
When rest of the world is ready to welcome.

It's you who think you should lose more
When the rest think you're perfect.

It's you who thought, Oh I've made fun of myself
When the rest thought that it was cute.

It's you picking up little imperfections in yourself,
And criticizing for that
While the rest were busy praising your uniqueness.

And when you felt alone,
It was you who thought maybe you're not lovable
While there was someone waiting up for you.

And the times when you felt depressed
And you didn't know the reason why.
It was you who could not rose above that
While the one depressed are every second trying to be happy.

My Friend it's you, you need to change
And not the world which you're always blaming.

THAT'S WHY I WONDER YOU SAY

Sometimes I just fall down as I want you to pull me up again.
I know what it's like to be strong !
So you can't label me a coward.

When emotions are bursting out inside you
They all want to come out and celebrate
But you know they shouldn't
So you trap them inside only
And they get all messed up, all mixed up.
How can any color mixed with black
Can result into a lighter shade ?
And so when they all mix up
All that remains is grey in color.
That grey lava, ready to burst out
And you have only a wall of smile to keep it in
Then you have to make sure that wall is strong enough
Strong enough to hold it in
Without cracking a bit.

And that's why
I wonder you say, You smile beautiful.

When all you have to do
Is take it out that is trapped inside
Maybe little a little in a while
But maybe little a little is not a thing
And all it require is to let flow as a whole
And that's the only thing the other lack
The thing to take it all down in

And maybe that's why
I wonder you say, I'm lost.

Akanksha Shrivastava

STAND A LITTLE MORE

If you think you're lost
Don't worry buddy
Something great is awaiting you.

Let me tell you that this is a journey
Whose destination you don't know
You're gonna extract everything out in the way only

Those little struggles
Those never ending nights
Sometimes frustrating
Sometimes delight

In the end of this unnamed journey
You're gonna come out loving yourself
You're gonna come out strong
The connection you must have made with your soul
Will then gonna be a precious bond.

But whenever you feel like falling down
Or you can't stand anymore
Stand ! Stand a little more
Find a Chair and then sit down
But only to get up again.
Don't just fall down on your face.

I AM AFRAID TO CLOSE MY EYES

The room is dark enough
And I am afraid to close my eyes
I have come so far that now I'm afraid to face that darkness again.

Are you listening ?
I remember feeling lost there
I almost lost my way out
I cried, I shouted, I screamed !
But I guess all that was inside.

I somehow chased the light
Igniting the way out.
And when I opened my eyes
I was relaxed to see you by my side.

But this time you won't be there
Maybe when I open my eyes there still will be dark.
As so the room is dark enough
And I am afraid to close my eyes.

Akanksha Shrivastava

I STAYED UP ALL NIGHT

And then suddenly I woke up!
I woke up in the middle of night.

For the very first time,
I was afraid to close my eyes again.
I was afraid that there is nothing left to dream
I was blank.

Staring up the ceiling
Trying not to close my eyes
I stayed up all night.
Blinking, counting patterns, acting scenarios
And trying not to sleep.

IT WILL ALL BE OKAY!

From all the people
To whom I've shared my story.
This is the response I received,
"You don't look like the person who've been through all this."
"You look Happy ! "

Well that's the key, people!
You will have to stop whining about it
And be Happy around.
As every single person out there
Is carrying his story
Some on the face, some on the shoulder and some hiding it in the
heart
Behind that cheerful face.
And a happy face, spreads a hopeful ray
To every person you smile upon
Saying, "I am with you
I know what you're going through
So let's Smile, It will all be Okay."

WHAT IF ?

There was a time,
When you were traveling on the road
And there came a junction
You wanted to take that turn
You knew about the destination
But not more than the path of the other way
And once a wise man said that the journey is more important than
the destination
And maybe that's why
That's why you kept moving in the same direction rather than taking
that turn.

But isn't it killing you now ?
What would have happened if you took that way ?
That it may have been a whole new experience
Maybe then you would have been able to tell your own stories of
adventure
Rather than telling how you cope up with the path millions have
traveled before.
Maybe you've been lost there somewhere.

But what if you've found yourself there ?
What if ?
All that's with you now is this question only.
Poking you around.

What if ?

SAY CHEESE!

Maybe you're not happy inside
Maybe you're not liking it
Inside you are running away from yourself

But let's just take a moment
Sit in a comfortable position
And smile, Smile for a picture
Because pictures say a lot !
Maybe just from the outside, but they do

So years later from now,
When you look this picture and try to recollect the moment
You won't end up remembering something you shouldn't
A happy picture will remind you of a happy moment.

Say Cheese !

YOUR SET OF MISTAKES

Do you have your set of mistakes?
Like, When you look back
You can say,
I admit I made a mistake there
And I learnt.
I think we all must have our mistakes
Our set of mistakes to be precise
Some unique from others
Which then later on makes you what you are today.
And then the stories,
Which you can narrate to others
Like a bravery tale or a funny one
And maybe those stories can help people to understand you in a
better way
Your fears, your obsessions, your way of living in total.

So next time when you meet someone new
Or want to know someone better
Ask their stories and help them to discover if they cannot recollect.
Ask them,
What are your set of mistakes ?

CITY THAT NEVER SLEEPS

A note to a city that never sleeps:

It's been more than an year now that I've met you
You've been amazing everyday
Your liveliness, your people made me fall in love with myself
You never stop, you never sleep
Someone somewhere is weaving his dream with the trust in you
everyday
You teaches us how to survive
"To live" to be precise.
When the rain falls to your floor
Everything suddenly becomes so magical
Everybody feels likes their life is a film
And the most dreamy part is now happening
Peeping out the window.
People love you, but you love them more I'll say
Your beauty, life, courage amazes me.
I'm happy to be here.
Let's keep counting.

Akanksha Shrivastava

LOVE STAYS

Love doesn't end just like that,
It fades away if not taken care of.

I've seen love staying,
And staying there for long.
No matter how many mistakes you make
They'll take care of you,
They'll take care of your trust in them,
That whenever you fail or deviate
They'll shower you with love
And not leave you believing this is how it is going to end.
They may not wander around all the time
But all you need to do is ask,
And you will find them standing beside you
And so I believe in love !
And being patient enough to see it nurturing.

YOUR DAY AWAITS

And when I realize that I can end it all by just opening my eyes.
Whatever was bothering me was all just in my mind.
Running around, escaping from the reality
Building up the scenarios
I realized,
People can only contribute to your story
In the way you want them to
But the summary is in your hands
You can suffer all along the time
Or you can make it a happy one.

I stopped listening to that unconscious mind of mine.
Because it was causing me my peace
And now I can hardly recall all that
But whenever I do.. that all looks far away and foolish too.

So here I am
Shouting your name again and again
Wake up ! Open your eyes !
Open those curtains, let the light in.
Stand... Your day awaits.

DRUNK ENOUGH ?

I don't know even now
To what limit should I drink
So that I can let it all out at once
Everytime I tried, I failed

I remember I was thinking
Should I say ?
Isn't it too cliche ?
Am I drunk enough ?
I don't think so.
Let's have another toast
Okay so.
Maybe now ?
Am I ready now ?
Let's start it. Say it. Let it out. You're drunk. You can say it now.
Or maybe I can't
I'm drunk enough, but also I'm conscious enough
Conscious enough to think that they'll judge
They won't understand
They won't listen
They're drunk.

So once again, here I am
Drunk. Sitting silently in the corner. Continuously battling in my
mind
Should I say ? Am I drunk enough now ?

ISN'T IT SELFISH ?

Isn't it selfish ?
To think about yourself only
And not the people around
"I love myself"
We've been drowned in so deep into this emotion
That now we've stopped caring about anything else
We'll do what we want
What we love
Without even caring about the consequences on others.
They do matter,
Specially when those are the people you love
Or you once loved.

Ever found yourself in a scenario
Where you thought that you were an important part of someone's
life
And then all of a sudden
They decides to love themselves
And left ?

Aren't we as a generation lacking something ?
Something that binds everyone together
We all want to get out of the cage
And fly away alone
Pity we are not having people around us
People whom we love and care about
People whom we unknowingly left somewhere behind
Because we wanted to achieve what we have now
We've achieved it very well
But pity, we have no one to celebrate it with and be happy about.

Akanksha Shrivastava

GETTING LOST IN THE MAZE

I am standing right now
I can sit beside you
Or I can put my head in your lap
As you say !
So that you can take a walk with your fingers
In the streets of my hair
Slipping through the skin
Making geometric or jumbled shapes

Wait, let me keep it on your shoulder
You can put that arm of yours
Going across the way of my shoulder
To the other end of my head
And you can take me to sleep
We won't talk, we won't sing
We won't be up for long
I'll be closing my eyes
While you be wandering around
With your fingers taking a walk
Or better getting lost
In the maze of my hair.

FLY AWAY

One day I want to leave everything behind
Every single ounce of worry in me
I want to drop that hard to the ground
Careless, Carefree, I want to fly away
On my own, for my own.

I want to see how this world looks like
How does it actually looks like !

I want to feel that air flapping on my face
Pumping itself hard into my hair.
I want to feel that every drop of rain
Before it rolls down my face.
I want to discover that laughter
That a baby makes for no reason
One day, I want to leave everything behind
Breaking all these barriers and travel alone
One day, I want to break free
On my own, for my own.

BETTER WALK AWAY

We have come a long way
But I better walk away.
For what's there trapped inside
Is so dark and dense to fight
I've felt it, I've held it
And so as we've now reached that door
But I won't let you get inside
Just in the desire of setting it free
And breathing a much lighter breeze
I cannot let you walk there naked

All of it is getting on me now
As we are heading closer, much closer
And all I can feel is cold, numb and grey.
How can I be so selfish
I cannot do this to you
You better leave now
For I'm staying here a little longer this time
You go out there, shine bright
And I'll be watching from here, gazing and fight.

YOU ARE SUFFOCATING

When the only time you spend with yourself
Is when you dream
And you often feel trapped in that too
My dear, you are suffocating !

When all you want is to scream out loud
Loud enough to let everything out
And then you find yourself still
Just thinking about all this
My dear, you are suffocating !

And if you find yourself
Writing it all out
Releasing it all through the ink of pen
and not talking about it
Oh dear, You are suffocating.

Akanksha Shrivastava

DEAR CARETAKER

Running far away from my own existence
Trying not to go in light to hide from my own shadow.
To stand up on the toes
And feeling that air flapping on my face
My hair singing along the waves
And an ear to ear smile.
I've come a long way

And now if you are asking me to sit down
and close every window in my sight
So I'm sorry, I cannot do that.

It happened a bit late
But now I have fallen in love with myself
And the air I am breathing in right now
Helps me cherish that love
So if you're asking me to tie my hair
And sit inside the walls
So I'm sorry, anything that will stop me from loving myself
I cannot do that
Maybe it is a way in which you want to show that you care.
But what you will never understand is that I may stop loving myself
in between those walls
I may stop breathing
I may die.
But dear caretaker, I want to live now !

LIVING FOR YOU

I am too tired to speak,
Please hold my hands and read my mind, will you ?

Those cold fingers of mine,
Can tell you how I feel.
Hold them tight, as my fast running heartbeat is ready to make them
shiver
Hold them tight, to gasp it all in.
I cannot say it with eyes,
They often sheds out the truth.
There is so much dark in here,
The moment it comes to my fingertips,
I may shy away and take my hands back.
As what they were going to pour down,
May shut the bright light there in you.
And that is what I am afraid of,
As that is what I am living for.

FINDING LOVE

Let us not wait to be perfect to find love
Start loving and caring for yourself
And love will eventually find you !

For the glow that comes to you
While selfcare and loving yourself
That's the glow that makes you realize
You are self sufficient, you're lovely !

Shout out to all the fading souls out there
Get up, be ready and take care of yourself
So that you can look upon a mirror and smile.

Find love,
Later in some individual
But the first in you.

FEAR OF FALLING DOWN

When you have seen the rock bottom of any situation
Only then you will crave for a solution
A ray of hope,
A jute rope,
Which can pull you up,
Or to which you can hold on to and climb up.

Only when the frog has seen all the corners of the well,
And realizes how much it is important to jump out.
Then he starts panicking,
And try making efforts in all directions to jump out and survive.

And when he reaches the top of the well with a rope thrown in,
He see the world above and the rock bottom straight down.
At that particular moment, he starts fearing the most
What if I fall ?
After seeing what's out there, now if I fall down,
And this rope has been pulled up,
Maybe I'll not be able to try again,
Maybe I won't survive.

SLOW POISON

Often we choose to settle down
When nothing is going as per you planned
You look out the window and chaos tries to get in
Things around you are falling apart
So you pause for a moment to pick up those pieces
You like to stay there for some time, to heal the bruises
But sometimes it is late when you realize
You have grown a habit of sitting there and watching the scars
Even if they were healed long time ago
You grabbed it and hide it in your heart
When you should have probably loosen and there itself let it go.
And then one day you get hit by a stone around
It hits you hard then slowly you realize
Even when you didn't want to
But you were, in your life, settled down.

BUILDING HOME

After years of shouting for help
And trying to get out, swim over
You realized that this is it.

So you built up a home there on the shore only
And started living there.
The more time passed by, the more you forgot how the world looks
like on the other side of sea.
Facing all the odds, finally when someone comes over to take you
back
You requests to take along all that you've built in years there.

But the boat is small,
Even if he wanted to, he cannot take it all in it.
So you choose to stay back,
As even though isolated, but you've made Home out of all those.
So from then on,
People often come to visit you,
You share laughter, cries, stories.
Each one of them proposed to take you out.
You smile, sometimes you cry a little
While explaining that this is my Home now.
And I am staying.

BRAVEST BATTLES

Hardest are the battles,
That are fought from inside.
When you can spend whole day,
Just staring at the ceiling and not remember what thinking.
When the spear of the darkness
Is tearing down your skin,
And the blood is shedding down
Like those tears from your eyes

Winning every time, winning it every night
You wash the tiredness from your face
And come out of the closet all smiling
As you're afraid to let them know,
About the chaos happening inside
Fearing about bursting it all out
You wrap it with a flower bow and leave it under the bed, hidden.
So that only you will be knowing,
Bravest are the battles, that are fought from inside.

CHOICE OF HAPPINESS

Often we forget
That sorrow is natural,
But Happiness is a choice !
When was the last time you chose to live it up and not crib about it ?

What have we become ?
We are finding pleasure in cribbing
When we don't want to put in much efforts.
We are surrounded by people like ourselves
Or we surrounded us with them while we overheard them cribbing
too.

Happy is the soul,
Who choose to not give it up.
And when you sit down for long in the break you took from fighting,
Often you find yourself,
Settling in the pool of depression, Drowning.

HOMESICK

I don't know if you can relate to it, but
Home is not just by the people who live there
But from those walls too which are considered merely a structure
That favorite bedside of yours
The corner where you found solitude and made all the tough
decisions
The stairs which takes you to the beautiful sky
The sound of closing gates and breeze getting in
The soft feel of bedsheet and its hugging comfort
That pure fragrance resting in the air
The smell of delicious food cooking in kitchen
The furniture kept and settled in a subtle way
And whenever I am homesick, I am craving for this comfort also
Along with the people who live there.

ECHO OF SILENCE

It came in my dream as a nightmare
And woke me up in the middle of the night.

Clashes of those things
Wandering in my mind
Shouting loudly
Internal echo so high
That it will burst in there only.

And now I am fully awake
In the middle of the night
Feeling lost
Thinking, is it worth it ?
Is it worth my peace ?

I am at that brim right now.
That if you take me out
I would want to sit beside you
My head on your shoulder
And eyes may keep blinking for long
And I may say nothing, For long.

As for what's trapped inside
That echo of shouting stress
Can only be ended
With an echo of silence, For long.

THE JAR THEORY

In this beautifully flawed world
You have created jars of limited size
And we all are flowing and resting in there

When we are not comfortable in the jar we have settled
We panic ! sometimes we melt down to adjust in the shape
Sometimes we gain the courage, to stand and flow outside
But just to get settled in the other jar
And this continues till you are not able to stand or flow.

All my life till now,
I am jumping from jar to jar.
I don't want to wait for my turn Where I may lose myself
When leaving every little piece of mine while flowing away from a jar
Sometimes I wish I had the courage to meltdown to that extent
Where I evaporate and be a part of the flowing air around.

LET THEM BE

If that fish is trying to climb the tree,
Let it be.
If that child is wanting to try new things,
Let him be.

If someone is actually trying something,
That makes them feel alive and happy,
Let them be.

Try finding happiness in realizing,
That at least they are taking a stand
And trying to make their lives better.

When all we are doing is cribbing
But afraid to actually get up and start

Try not mocking the souls,
Who flapped their wings and couldn't fly.
Instead be a witness to say, Oh he tried !

For you may never know,
Watching you laughing at them,
They may never stand and dare to dream again.
When it was just a run they needed,
Before they could fly away !

BRING ME BACK

Some days I feel like running,
Running and not knowing where to stop.
Past that regular lamppost
Away from that daily left turn
Till I don't remember why I started it in the first place.

And,
Some days I feel like not moving an inch,
Staring and staring anything in front of my eyes,
And not realizing that my mind was just blank all along.

In all these days,
I am crying out loud to reach out.
Asking to stop me from running so far,
Or maybe jerk me hard while I'm staring at something,
And bring me back.

STUBBORN CHILD

Watching you go near that cliff,
Taking a step back to fly away higher,
Often they try to convince you that,
Life till that cliff is much happier
And not after it.

It's so weird that,
They, who have never been there
Tries to make you believe that you are making a mistake.
But you, You stubborn child, I Love You !
You choose to go there anyway,
And you took responsibility of any lesson you may learn there.
May that be success or failure.
You will have a story to tell,
So that next time they cannot stop someone else like you,
To explore what is beyond that cliff.
So what you failed ?
Let them try,
Let them fail, fall, get up and try again.
And fly again.

Akanksha Shrivastava

TINY DROPS OF RAIN

It is so beautiful,
How those tiny drops can fill this city with happy colors,
How every music in ears along with these rains,
Can make you feel like you are in a fairy tale,
Or dancing to the tunes of piano playing in a farland.

How it makes you fall in love with yourself all over again.
Walking holding that giant umbrella,
And feeling that little splash of raindrops on your face,
Smiling to the happy songs for no reason at all.

Often you may find me sitting silently alone,
Sipping up tea,
Watching rain drops racing their way down the glass,
And behind it this city resting like a scenery.

A different sweet fragrance travels all over with cold breeze,
Playing with your hair,
And you don't even bother to tie them up.
Leaving calmness in your eyes,
Leaving everything relatively beautiful and poetic.

WELL THEN, I LIKE YOU TOO

When we have talked all day,
And you felt a little spark in between us,
And if you say that you think you like me !
I will take the lead and suggest you to wait till the Sun goes down,
And the silent night comes around.
Since O'dear !
I can go somewhat ambiguous, somewhat lost
Also I may end up questioning my own existence,
When the world goes silent and the thoughts come alive.
There is some dark magic in the aura of night,
Which takes me to take a deep dive into life.
So we will have questions,
We may have answers.
There will be you,
And there will be me, but a slightly different me.
So if after that night,
You say that you think you like me.
Well then I like you too.

Akanksha Shrivastava

LAST LOVE

In the world with songs full of first love,
I want to be your last love.
And wish that you can be mine too.

Just close your eyes for a moment and dive in to see,
How blissful it is to be someone's first,
But, how fierce is it to be their last and forever !

Like you are passing through a way, changing lanes
And decide to stay there for a while,
Without even exploring other paths, you say
I can stay here, I can settle here now.

Don't you see ?
How beautiful it is ?
To love again, and realize
Yes, now this is the person I can spend my life with.
This is where I can happily reside.

STORIES, FACES WON'T TELL

Face should not be considered as the symbol of one's soul
As what resides behind that face are a lot of stories
Stories they don't want to tell you
Or they think that maybe you won't understand
Stories they don't want to be left as a narration for you
Believe me, no one other than those faces want to be understood
and loved
But what they fear is to explain you what's happening inside them
When even they don't understand it
And how many efforts they have made to get rid of it

Yes sometimes I purposely prepare a bath with a tub full of
insecurities
And drown in deep, playing with the bubble of scenarios in my head
I cannot make you understand that why I like making a home there
After everytime I damage it while leaving
No one likes to be trapped in the clouds of dullness
But that cave of darkness calls me to itself
And I as always reach out to rest there and feel like home.
So here I am making it all clear to you
I know it's hard for you to understand all this
But all I am asking is you to sit beside me
Let my floating mind know that you're here with me
So that I won't swim far away from us
And not blame it for having such miserable thoughts
As it too is tired of traveling this much again and again
And let's hope that what's there inside should be transparent enough
to reflect on the face outside.

THE SKY IS PINK

There are some movies which entertains you for a while,
And then there are some which stays with you a lifetime.
'The Sky is Pink' is the movie which will give warmth to your heart.
How beautifully they portrayed journey of a family going through a lot,
Never in that story came a moment where they let you pour pity on them,
All you are left with a feeling like, Wow such a brave soul.
How gracefully they painted a picture which was happy and courageous at the same time,
Like we cried for their efforts to not make it sad and fearful.
So beautifully they taught us that letting go is a part of life,
And it's not necessary that goodbyes should be devastating.
Their story lead us to believe that life is not to worry about death,
But to embrace the last moments you have and make them count.
This story now have a special place in my heart,
And whenever I will feel like giving up I'll surely come back for what this story has taught me.
It is so wonderful to think about that it is just one story
And we have many more like this around us.
About people who chose to stand tall and look death in the eye,
And left other around them in awe of courage they showed.

CALCULATED LOVE

Spreading the carpet of affection,
How easily we start imprinting it with the colors of our conditions,
Colors which you both want in it to be.
Sometimes discussing and sometimes arguing about narrowing it
down to one,
So that the carpet may be weaved beautifully and lasts longer.

And after all this time spent in weaving and coloring the carpet
together
We may leave it there and start searching for a different partner to
color it with
Because the carpet didn't come out to be so gorgeous with the colors
you both picked up together to fill in.

After all this you say you were then in love,
Wherein often you forget that what all efforts you put in there were
estimated
And what you say was affection was not more than just calculated
love.

Akanksha Shrivastava

DON'T WANT TO BELONG

The one thing
That I'm afraid of
Is to be trapped here, for long
And realizing it lately.

And for that sake only
I want to fly away, Not so far
Just distant enough from its sight
Close enough from its smell
Paranoid, isn't it ?

The air that I'm feeling, keeping me alive
Is the one helping not to suffocate
I want to live here
But don't want to belong.

NOT ALONE!

As they say,
Every morning you're not able to get up from the bed.
But I am !
I daily get up the very first time my eyes open.
I can't close them again.
And I'll buckle up and will get ready for work.
As spending a whole day with myself
Scares me more, than spending it with different people around me.
I can have a conversation in my mind while being with people
But no.. not alone.

Akanksha Shrivastava

WELCOME SADNESS

Crossing the way,
Someone asked me, How are you ?
Wonder why I started telling about you,
Your existence.
And there you got me again
We haven't met in months
Well, not a pleasant memory you are
But I am there now, stuck.
Welcome back Buddy!
I am ready to sink in.

FOR THOSE EYES

Look into those eyes
you will see craving
for that last piece of meal
that never got expressed.

Go a little deep
There you will find fear for you
that came out as restrictions.

And all that,
All that covered under the layer of wrinkles.
So if you ever feel like giving up
Try again for those eyes.

Akanksha Shrivastava

YOU ARE ALIVE

Hey,
Hey you !
Shrinking in the blanket of sorrow
Come on now, hold my hand
and throw away that blanket of yours.
I am here to make you remind
You have missed an opportunity,
But there is a lot more to find
As life is happily heading forward
and those are just dead residing behind
And I know that,
You are alive.

SHE IS A MYSTERY

Untangling her curls, she is sitting on the chair.
Sipping up the coffee, oh I love those hair.
Staring her looks, she caught me today.
Winking with a smile, oh she made my day.
My friend, she is a mystery
And I am rediscovering her everyday.

Playing with her fingers, she is watching movie.
Weeping lightly in the flow, oh I love those eyes.
Desiring her soul, she caught me again.
Blushing in her way, she threw a popcorn at me,
Oh she drives me crazy.
Yes, she is a mystery
And I am rediscovering her everyday.

Portraying her makeup, she is getting ready.
Looking beautiful in that dress, oh I love that body.
Praising through my eyes,
You know ? She caught me again.
Cackling lovely, she tapped on my head
Oh she took me away.
Oh yeah, she is a mystery
And I am rediscovering her everyday.

Akanksha Shrivastava

LET'S NOT JUST TALK TODAY

Hey there,
Are you listening dear?
It may sound a little weird to say,
But let's not just talk today.

I want to wander in these eyes of yours,
We can swim in the depths of the oceans hidden.
Or maybe just peep into our hearts so driven.
But let's not just talk today.

I want to solve those tangled mysteries of your hair.
And you may pretend like you don't know the way.
Little and little I'll free that air,
You trapped in them to fly away one day.
Now, it may look like an easier way,
But let's not just talk today.

I want to walk with you along,
on the side of a beach somewhere.
We will see the sun waving goodbye for long,
while kissing the sea right there.
It may not sound like seizing the day,
But let's not just talk today.

TICK TOCK TICK TOCK

You know how it feels ?
When there is a time bomb,
ticking inside you.
And it will explode if exposed.

So there you are,
Lying down in the blanket of helplessness,
on the bed of suffering,
Mumbling that tune.
Tick tock tick tock tick tock…

Akanksha Shrivastava

KNOCK KNOCK

Dear People,
Now whenever depression knocks in
Do not stand back and freeze!
Or close all the curtains and weep.

Switch on the lights,
Yes, the pretty fairy lights too
Open the door,
Greet him with a smile,
Make him comfortable,
Offer some tea,
And tell him that,
Life is beautiful !

AND THEN…

I saw him today
Unlike other days,
He approached me this time.
We talked for hours,
I then decided to say what I wanted to say years ago,
Yes, I was ready.

But then suddenly,
Everything started becoming blur,
It all started fading away
His voice became hard to listen.
And then,
I woke up !

Akanksha Shrivastava

I FEEL LIKE I'M HOME

Psst..
Hey listen !
Yes you !
Sitting there in front of me
All cuddled up and smiling.
All these years,
I've been searching for a shoulder to rest upon
And a hand to hold on for long.
In the past few days I realized

Battling around all day,
Struggling to express it all out.
Finally when I come back to you
When I feel I'm safe,
I'm happy enough to say it all,
I feel like I'm Home.

When you stand giant in front of me,
And I immerse my head in your chest
With your arms around
Trying to contain it all within
With that mind so in peace
And heart at it's rest
I feel like I'm Home.

Gradually while talking,
I rest my head on your shoulder
Lifting up my head when I look up to that smile
And realize it is there now in my life
All the stress these eyes hold sheds in a while
And shying a little then I admit
I now feel like, I'm Home.

SHOULD HAVE NOT

There come some days,
In all of our lives

When after a long day,
Or maybe a long week,
You lay down on the bed,
Close your eyes to relax,
And see nothing but chaos building up.

And you have to pluck out strands,
One by one,
To untangle that web.

Sometimes you make it a straight thread easily
And sometimes you end up messing it all
And dropping it to the ground the very moment.
Leaving you nothing but pale and cold
Staring the blank wall
Dare not to move, you think
Should have waited some more time,
Should have not closed my eyes.

A PLACE

I am at a place, so peaceful and secure
Streets are in silence, no noise at more.
Doing what never want to, now has to be done
Feeling what never hope so, now has to be opt.

The life with peace is here this way,
Which I have to choose, leaving something away.

Your dreams will have to shatter to get this life,
Your eyes must not rise so high, to take its pie
You have to limit yourself to get in this place,
So peaceful and secure but still leave some trace.

A place full of boredom and things I do not want to do,
A place whole secure, but with internal Mindstorms.

This is a place enough for dumb screams,
I am at a place, miles and miles away from my dreams.